An opinionated guide

T0244961

BERLIN

Written by
LYDIA WINTER

Orangerie Neukölln (no.29)

INFORMATION IS DEAD. LONG LIVE OPINION.

Everything you could ever want to know about Berlin is available online. For free. There is no point to this guidebook. Right?

Wrong. The point of this guidebook is to give you the best opinion, not the most information. We've distilled Berlin, brutally, perhaps unfairly – but brilliantly – to a short and satisifying list of the very best places to go.

That may upset you. But wait, here's something even worse. We are an east London publisher, so what do we know? Well, aside from the fact that Lydia, the writer, lives in Berlin and our editor Zoë lived there too, we see a synergy with the east London that we know and love: the creativity, the diversity, the slightly grubby concrete... oh, and the coffee. Trust us or don't – just try these places.

Berlinische Galerie (no.48)
Right: DARK MATTER (no.54)

ORA (no.3)
Left: Ita Bistro (no.26)

The Hoxton, Charlottenburg (no.76)

MORE THAN EUROPE'S
PARTY CAPITAL

Freedom: that's the feeling conjured by Berlin. Freedom for anyone to be who they want to be, and dress how they want to dress. Tattooed, pierced, all-black leather clothing, colourful clothing, no clothing; skinheads, mohawks, mullets, jagged fringes. It's a physical freedom felt in the wide streets, high ceilings and possibility of getting a seat in a good restaurant without weeks of planning. A freedom that could see you cycling to Markthalle Neun (no.13) on Saturday morning for organic *Spargel* (white asparagus), then dancing for 12 hours straight to trance remixes of Sean Paul and Nelly Furtado in the afternoon.

It's a city brimming with cultural offerings. Berlin is home to one of the world's greatest orchestras at the Philharmonie (no.52) and a techno scene under UNESCO protection – experience it for yourself at OHM Gallery (no.88) or head to waterside Club der Visionäre (no.81) for impeccable house music curation. As for exhibitions, KW Institute (no.49) and the Boros Foundation (no.59) will challenge your perspectives, while the Berlinische Galerie (no.48) shows you how far Berlin's influence extends. The legendary nightlife is one of the first things people associate with Berlin, but it's time to start thinking of the city as far more than 'Europe's party capital'.

You can't explore Berlin without experiencing its 20th-century scars – in the former US listening station at Teufelsberg (no.69) or the two bunkers-turned-viewing platforms at Volkspark Humboldthain (no.72). The Berlin Wall trail is marked with remnants and memorials, while brass stones set between cobblestones across the city name the victims of World War II. This history has left its mark on Berlin's inhabitants, too. In the aftermath of Stasi surveillance, Berliners remain staunch protectors of their own privacy. Cash is still king in Berlin, and this, coupled with a general distrust of big tech, accounts for the hundreds of 'CASH ONLY' signs you'll see hanging around the city. Suspicious of newcomers but fundamentally warm-hearted, it can take time cracking a Berliner's gruff exterior (also known as *Berliner Schnauze*) – but once you do, the rewards are as sweet as the cinnamon buns from Zeit für Brot (no.27).

When former Berlin mayor Klaus Wowereit called Berlin 'poor but sexy' in 2003, the city's economy was lagging behind those of other European capitals and Berlin was still battling the cultural and political aftermath of reunification. Some 20 years on, Berlin has evolved again and the economy and restaurant scene are catching up, bringing plenty of excellent small plates and natural wine spots like Otto (no.18) and Barra (no.17). As in other formerly unruly and artistic cities, with gentrification comes the fear of losing the rebellious spirit that was once its allure. But here, a strong protest culture remains, with every 1 May a bank holiday dedicated to demonstrations supporting workers' rights (and rowdy street parties). And even though the rent cap declared in 2021 was eventually repealed by Germany's constitutional court, it showed the strength of Berlin's housing movement and left-wing parties.

You can still find that irresistible Berlin spirit if you know where to look, and that's exactly what this book is about: showing you the pockets still fizzing with tantalising possibility.

In the 2003 film *Goodbye Lenin*, the protagonist tries to shield his socialist mother from news about the fall of the Berlin Wall when she emerges from an eight-month coma. One warm evening, as he and a date dangle their legs over a building ledge, he muses, 'Summer came, and Berlin was the most beautiful place on Earth. We had the feeling we were standing in the centre of the world.'

This moment captures Berlin at its best: big skies and sensational sunsets on Tempelhofer Feld (no.65); long, slow twilights that set the scene for endless dancing; swimming naked in one of the city's thousand lakes on a sweltering summer day. To truly experience Berlin, you have to immerse yourself in it – clubs, history, *Schnauze* and all.

Lydia Winter
Berlin, 2024

CONTRIBUTORS

About Hoxton Mini Press

Hoxton Mini Press is small indie publisher based in east London. We're dedicated to making beautiful books about art and culture that are accessible to everyone. We DO NOT make e-books, and when our books arrive from the printer we SMELL the paper. In an excessively digital age, we trust in the joy of the physical book. We hope this copy will rest neatly on a fine wooden shelf and perhaps be kept for your great-great-grandchild.

About Lydia Winter

Lydia Winter is a Berlin-based journalist and editor, with writing in the likes of *FT Weekend*, *HTSI*, *Condé Nast Traveller*, *Courier* and more. Half-German and raised in the UK by a 'real Berliner', she's spent a lifetime balancing German directness with English politeness, and once ate 12 *Knödel* (German dumplings) in one sitting.

A PERFECT WEEKEND

Friday night

Ring in the weekend with swish cocktails and vegan antipasti in the beautiful Orangerie (no.29). For something more substantial, mosey over to Barra (no.17) for natural wine and small plates. If it's summer, catch the tail end of sunset on Tempelhofer Feld (no.65).

Saturday morning

Start your day with breakfast atop the Reichstag (no.53) for smoked salmon, a close-up of Norman Foster's dome and free access to the spiral walkway.

Saturday lunch

Schöneberg's Winterfeldtplatz Markt (no.66) offers a taste of west Berlin's boho spirit. Amble through the market, pick up some ceramics and a *Krabbenbrötchen* (shrimp roll), before strolling along famous boulevard Kurfürstendamm to KaDeWe (no.35) to gawp at the gourmet food hall.

Saturday afternoon

Head to Fotografiska (no.46), a former artists' squat, now gallery, where you can take your *Sekt* (sparkling wine) with you while gazing at world-leading contemporary photography. The afternoon is for browsing Mitte's various boutiques, before engaging in the German ritual of coffee and cake at SOFI (no.9).

Saturday evening

Pair open-fire cooking at Kramer (no.15) with experimental cocktails at Wax On (no.86) in Neukölln. If you're in the mood for a late one, Club der Visionäre (no.81) will easily take you through to the early hours, or head to ://about blank (no.87) for a proper night out.

Sunday brunch

Your reserves will be depleted after hours of dancing, so Annelies (no.5) and their leaning tower of pancakes are just the ticket. Top up on vitamin D and try to bring your circadian rhythm back to normality with a walk through Görlitzer Park.

Sunday afternoon

The sensory explosion of Boxhagener Platz (no.68) flea market will certainly wake you up – or slope off to book- and coffee shop Shakespeare & Sons (no.31) to curl up in an armchair with a lox bagel with jalapeno cream cheese.

Sunday evening

Zoom over to Prenzlauer Berg's wide, cobbled streets for a cleansing sushi dinner at Omoni (no.23), followed by a few chilled drinks at *Kneipe* Macke Prinz (no.83). In need of something more restorative? Book a late-night swim and sauna session in Hotel Oderberger's (no.74) stunning vaulted pool.

BEST FOR...

Casual eating

'Casual' is a mood that Berlin does well, but that doesn't make the food any less creative. Knödelwirtschaft (no.1) is a case in point, dressing up traditional German dumplings. In Neukölln, Gazzo's (no.16) pizzas (with regionally sourced burrata) elicit queues around the block and La Bolognina (no.25) dishes up plates of mortadella-filled ravioli to a vinyl soundtrack.

Meals to impress for dates (and mates)

The reign of pork and potatoes is at an end. Prenzlauer Berg's beautiful Otto (no.18) demonstrates a winning combination of seasonal tasting menus and natural wine, while spice lovers will appreciate Sri Lankan-inspired dishes at Sathutu (no.24). For a meal to remember, Kramer (no.15) turns up the creative heat with its wood-fired inventions.

Art in the right places

Creativity abounds in Berlin, where gallery spaces are often as inventive as the works within them. Make a day of it at squat-turned-photography institute Fotografiska (no.46), or visit König Galerie (no.57), which occupies a striking Brutalist church. The singular Boros Foundation (no.59), a former Nazi HQ/Soviet prison/night club, perfectly captures the city's transformational spirit.

The great outdoors

Contrary to its reputation for endless concrete, Berlin is bursting with green spaces and lakes. Tempelhofer Feld's (no.65) history and community space secure its iconic status. Northwards, Rehberge (no.71) offers sprawling wilderness and a 1920s lido. In west Berlin, Krumme Lanke's (no.63) swimmable waters are an irresistible tonic on scorching summer days.

Music for everyone's ears

Berlin's music heritage reverberates from every corner. But it's not all techno raves: the Philharmonie (no.52) is home to one of the world's best orchestras, Tresor's sister club OHM (no.88) offers experimental musical curation and waterside Club der Visionäre (no.81) is a temple for minimal house.

Bread winners

Knowing where to get your daily bread is a must, and Berlin's bakeries are bound to impress. Lust after La Maison's (no.7) perfectly laminated pastries and bedazzling baked goods, or seek out SOFI's (no.9) offerings made with ancient grains and regeneratively farmed flour.

Indie heroes

Given you've got this book in your hands, you're likely to love do you read me?! (no.32), a celebration of print. Bookworms and bagel addicts will appreciate Shakespeare & Sons (no.31). Audiophiles can make a pilgrimage to record store Hard Wax (no.30), while concept shop Voo (no.38) offers fashion, a deli and exhibitions all in one space.

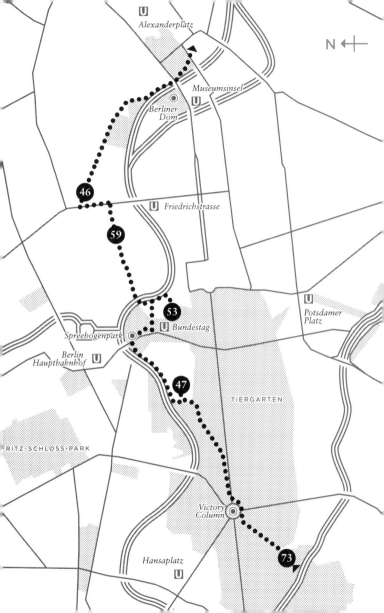

N

Alexanderplatz

Museumsinsel

Berliner
Dom

46

Friedrichstrasse

59

Potsdamer
Platz

53

Spreebogenpark

Bundestag

Berlin
Hauptbahnhof

47

TIERGARTEN

FRITZ-SCHLOSS-PARK

Victory
Column

73

Hansaplatz

WALK 1

Dive into the city's art scene with a riverside walk
past the cream of Berlin's cultural crop

Fuel up for a full day of cultural immersion with brunch at *Café am Neuen See* **73**, where plentiful egg dishes get things off to a cracking start. Stroll through iconic park Tiergarten, past the gilded *Victory Column** (climb the 285 steps to the top if you're feeling energetic) and land on the river path, reaching museum *Haus der Kulturen der Welt* **47** just in time for a coffee at Weltwirtschaft, their waterside restaurant. Follow the Spree around the riverbend through *Spreebogenpark**, to spy Norman Foster's glittering dome perched atop the *Reichstag* **53**. From here, your day could go two ways: another cultural pitstop at bunker-turned-private gallery *Boros Foundation* **59** and/or glossy photography institution *Fotografiska* **46** or, if that seems a step too far, stick to the river. You'll soon find the Gothic silhouette of the *Berliner Dom**, which still bears blemishes from World War II. Cross the river here and end your day in the ancient Nikolaiviertel neighbourhood, which could be lifted straight out of *Hansel and Gretel*.

Walking time: 1.5 hours, 7km
Total time with stops: 4–5 hours
*Not in guidebook: more info online

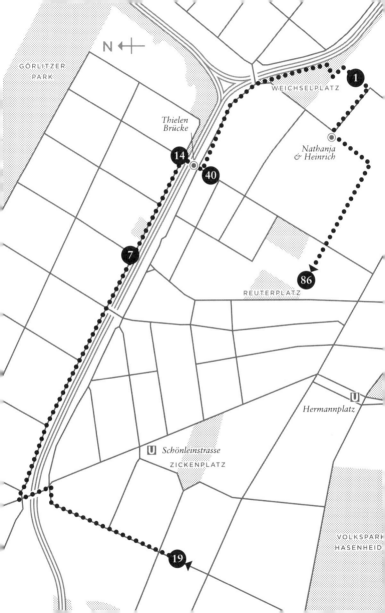

WALK 2

*Grab your stretchy pants for a day of eating, drinking
and carousing in Kreuzberg and Neukölln*

Start at *St. Bart* ❶❾ for a slap-up Sunday lunch before embark-
ing on a post-prandial stroll up Gräfestrasse, crossing
over Kottbusser Brücke and turning right onto canal path
Paul-Lincke-Ufer. Walk along the tree-shaded riverbank to
bakery *La Maison* ❼, where pastry is an art form and the
croque monsieur sandwiches are mind-blowing. If you can't
find a place to sit on the terrace, perch by the boules park to
watch the quietly competitive games. Continue along the
path to *Pavillon am Ufer* ❶❹ for an Aperol spritz and cross the
river again at *Thielenbrücke**, a popular sunset spot, to find
second-hand emporium *The Good Store* ❹❶. Once you're done
lusting over the curated apparel, walk along Maybachufer and,
if you've still got stomach space, sit down for a contemporary
take on traditional German dumplings at *Knödelwirtschaft's* ❶
Neukölln outpost. If it's drinks you're after, turn west up
Ossastrasse towards Neukölln's Reuterkiez for the most experimental list of negronis you'll ever encounter at *Nathanja &
Heinrich** or centrifuged cocktails at *Wax On* ❽❻.

Walking time: 45 minutes, 3.5km
Total time with stops: 3–5 hours
*Not in guidebook: more info online

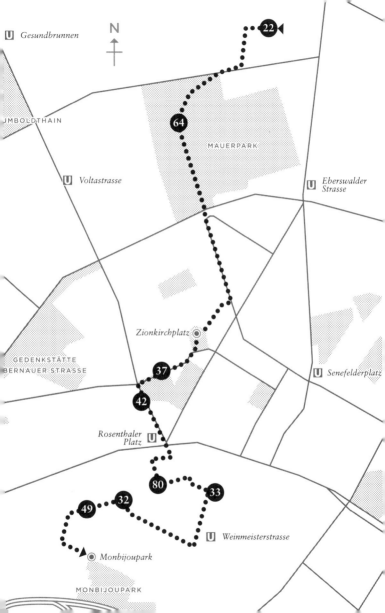

U *Gesundbrunnen*

N

JMBOLDTHAIN

U *Voltastrasse*

64

MAUERPARK

U *Eberswalder Strasse*

GEDENKSTÄTTE
BERNAUER STRASSE

Zionkirchplatz

U *Senefelderplatz*

37

42

Rosenthaler Platz U

80

33

49 32

U *Weinmeisterstrasse*

Monbijoupark

MONBIJOUPARK

22

WALK 3

A day taking in Prenzlauer Berg at its most enchanting

Turn any preconceptions of Berlin as a grey concrete jungle upside down with an exploration of Prenzlauer Berg's tree-lined boulevards and cobbled streets. Start with a trout bagel or luxurious French toast with rhubarb at *Estelle* **22**. Walk through *Mauerpark* **64** (and the flea market, if it's a Sunday) then trace the path where the Berlin Wall once stood until you reach Schwedter Strasse. Admire the pastel-coloured *Altbau* (old apartment) buildings then head southwest to cross *Zionskirchplatz**, where you'll see the church that became a centre for GDR opposition before Berlin's reunification. At the square's southwestern corner is Veteranenstrasse, where you'll pass irresistible design boutique *Maisinger* **37** – enter at your purchasing peril. Turn the corner and you'll find *Ocelot* **42** bookshop, before making your way to *Hackbarth's* **80** for a coffee. Wander Mitte's elegant shopping streets, setting your sights on superlative stationery store *R.S.V.P.* **33** and magazine shop *do you read me?!* **32** before heading to *KW Institute* **49** for the kind of conversation-starting exhibition you'll be thinking about for days. The final flourish? A *Späti* (corner shop) beer on the river in *Monbijoupark**.

Walking time: 1 hour, 5km
Total time with stops: 3–4 hours
*Not in guidebook: more info online

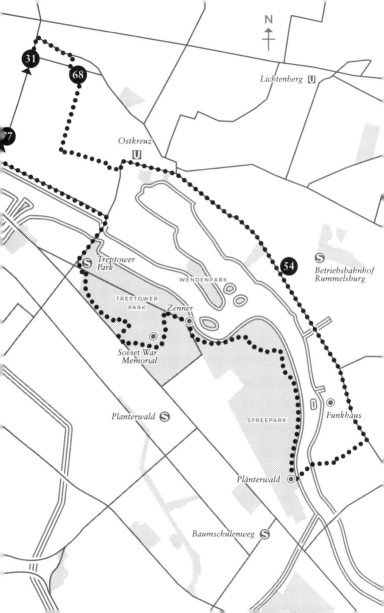

CYCLE 1

Fuel up in Friedrichshain before exploring Plänterwald Forest

Shakespeare & Sons **31** is the ideal springboard to load up on carbs and caffeine. If it's a Sunday, roll over to *Boxhagener Platz* **68**, one of Berlin's best flea markets. Then start your ride in earnest, cycling 4km to audiovisual exhibition *Dark Matter* **54**. Continue southwest along Köpenicker Chaussee and pass the *Funkhaus**, a former GDR broadcasting centre that's now a music venue (and semi-secret pizza spot). Turn right at Fritz-König-Weg and make for the river Spree. Hop on the ferry, which conveniently drops you off on the *Plänterwald** cycle path. Follow the route back towards town, keeping an eye out for otters. Arriving at the southernmost end of Treptower Park and lovely beer garden *Zenner**, grab a currywurst *mit Pommes* and quite possibly a beer. Pass the imposing columns of the *Soviet War Memorial**, then back onto the main road. Turn right when the park comes to an end, cross the river and turn left to reach Warschauer Strasse, looking out for the glowing signage of the *Michelberger Hotel* **77**, home to an excellent wine bar and cafe – go on, you've earned it.

Cycling time: 1 hour, 16km
Total time with stops: 2–3 hours
*Not in guidebook: more info online

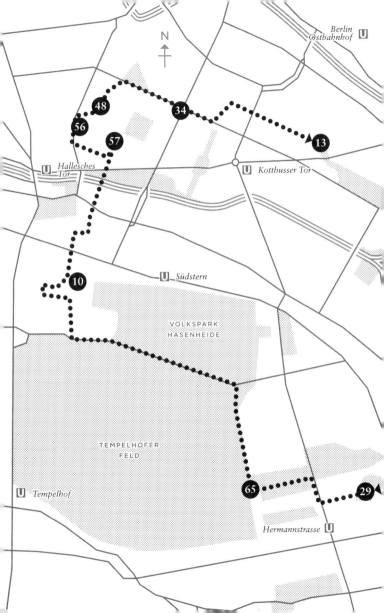

CYCLE 2

Tempelhofer Feld, Bergmannkiez and some of Berlin's best galleries

Start your day at *Orangerie* **29** in Neukölln (before 2:30pm, so you can try whichever lunch dish is on offer), then head directly to *Tempelhofer Feld* **65**, where wide, open skies and wholesome views of people skating, kiteboarding and cycling up and down the old runaways will warm the cockles of your heart. Join in or park up and linger a while, contemplating the silhouette of the old airport building, now a cultural space, or perhaps stumbling across a day party. Head to the northwestern corner, where you'll pop out into beautiful Bergmannkiez, home to schnitzel paradise *Felix Austria* **10**, before peddling north, over the Landwehrkanal, where you'll find a pocket of galleries and museums. Take your pick between repurposed Brutalist church *König Galerie* **57**, Berlin-inspired space *Berlinische Galerie* **48** or the *Jüdisches Museum* **56**. Hop back on your bike and up to busy Oranienstrasse, cycling east to Moritzplatz where you'll find one-stop arts-and-crafts shop *Modulor* **34**. From there, it's an easy stretch to *Markthalle Neun* **13** and Lausitzer Platz, both excellent spots for a bite to eat or a glass of wine.

Cycling time: 45 minutes, 11km
Total time with stops: 2–5 hours
*Not in guidebook: more info online

1

KNÖDELWIRTSCHAFT NORD

Traditional German cooking refined

German cuisine isn't famous for its sex appeal, but *hut ab* (hats off) to Knödelwirtschaft for turning a ball of steamed dough into something both delicious and intensely desirable. The traditional German dumpling is given a cunning 21st-century makeover, with seasonal varieties like asparagus *Knödel* (creating the most German duo you'll ever encounter), or a mushroom version for vegans, garnished with generous gratings of parmesan and a tart green salad. It helps that the beautiful Prenzlauer Berg outpost reflects the restaurant's blend of traditional and modern German style, with lofty ceilings, white-washed walls and an espresso-toned wood bar.

Stargarder Strasse 3, 10437
Nearest station: Schönhauser Allee
Other location: Neukölln
knoedelwirtschaft.de

2

SWORD MASTER NOODLE

Supersized Korean-style noodles and soups

White-tiled walls and scruffy seating keep all eyes on the open kitchen at this Korean street food-inspired noodle spot, where you'll see chefs hand-cutting every single noodle (hence the name). These Rapunzel-esque ribbons make their way into a short menu of soups and stews, headlined by the spicy seafood noodle soup. The signature dish earned its rep for a reason: generously packed with squid, mussels and clams floating in an oily red broth, it has a depth of flavour that leaves a lasting impression on the palate. For all the seriousness with regards to soup, there's still a playful streak – go to the toilet and you'll find a retro TV playing old-school Korean cartoons.

Dunckerstrasse 30, 10439
Nearest station: Prenzlauer Allee
instagram.com/swordmaster_noodle

3

ORA

Standout restaurant in a 19th-century pharmacy

The moment you step into Ora, you know you're in for something special. Occupying a former *Apotheke* (pharmacy) on Oranienplatz, the original carved woodwork and ceiling cornices create a dining space as beautiful as the food served within it. Don't be fooled by the elevated surrounds – Ora prides itself on refreshingly unpretentious cooking. You might eat a gussied-up hot dog daubed with apricot mustard and potato skin mayo served on a Japanese milk bread bun, or bream crudo with pickled kombu, turnips and a chilled smoked bone broth. Try to get a table at the back, where the view of the space makes it the best seat in the house.

Oranienplatz 14, 10999
Nearest station: Moritzplatz
ora.berlin

4

ROGACKI

Old-school deli and pre-war timewarp

Rogacki is a historic *Feinkost* (delicatessen), worth a visit as much for the plates of smoked and cured fish and potato rösti as it is for a taste of Berlin's history – it first opened in 1928. Under Art Deco-inspired spherical ceiling lights, glass deli counters display everything from baked goods and sausages to fish, still smoked in the huge on-site roasters. Charlottenburg's old guard come here to collect their weekly portion of pickled herring, and you'll often see them enjoying a glass of chilled Reisling and oysters, propping up high tables bedecked in lurid plastic green tablecloths. Head to the *Schlemmerecke* (or 'gourmand's corner') to munch your way through plates of cold cuts, served to you with a side of *Berliner Schnauze*.

Wilmersdorfer Strasse 145, 10585
Nearest station: Bismarckstrasse
rogacki.de

5

ANNELIES

OTT brunch crowned by Berlin's best pancakes

Trendy cafe meets creative brunch dishes at Annelies, where every plate makes for an eye-popping feast. King of them all are their fluffy pancakes, piled high in a gloriously wobbly tower and served in a puddle of maple syrup, topped with a perfect quenelle of cultured cream. Don't overlook the sourdough toast loaded with gratings of smoked egg yolk and crunchy fennel kimchi, or a vertigo-inducing sausage sandwich made with a pork patty, sesame pancake bun and American cheese, reminiscent of the fast food breakfast favourite. Visual appeal aside, this breakfast spot is genuinely superb, delivering its dishes against a backdrop of unvarnished wooden floors and concrete walls that puts the food centre stage.

Görlitzer Strasse 68, 10997
Nearest station: Görlitzer Bahnhof
anneliesberlin.com

6
JULIUS

Vaunted tasting menus and under-the-radar brunch

Whether it's an omelette or a 'micro-seasonal' (and micro-sized) dish of beetroot and umeboshi plums, this white-tiled corner in Wedding's Nettelbeck-platz presents dishes so exquisitely it almost feels a crime to eat them. An offshoot of Michelin-starred sensation Ernst, the experience here is no less meticulous. Japanese-influenced small plates and biodynamic wines dominate after dusk, but the best time to go is actually at brunch, when their pared-back menu features an exceptionally thick square of brioche French toast. The prices may be extravagant but the serene setting and the coffee, brewed by co-owner and master barista Shoji Hara, will encourage you to linger – even if the grey concrete of Wedding S-Bahn station does not.

Gerichtstrasse 31, 13347
Nearest station: Reinickendorfer Strasse
juliusberlin.de

7

LA MAISON

Lauded pastries and sandwiches worth the hype

La Maison's window is more enticing than a jewellery display case: burnished golden breads, glistening ruby-red danishes and cloud-like choux buns all jostle for space, making it hard to know where to look – but you'll have more than enough time as you wait in line for the takeaway hatch of this bakery on Paul-Lincke-Ufer. Collect your pastries, baguette and coffee (made with beans from Kreuzberg neighbour Vote) and watch the games at the boules courts, where locals face off in fierce competitions. You can also linger on La Maison's terrace, where you'll find appropriately Gallic-looking red-and-white chairs and teeny tiny round tables that are far too small for the number of sandwiches you'll want to order.

Paul-Lincke-Ufer 17, 10999
Nearest station: Schönleinstrasse
lamaison.berlin

8

BONANZA
COFFEE ROASTERS

OG Berlin coffee roaster and cafe

Bonanza were one of the first bean-focused cafes and roasteries in Berlin and, even more impressive, they've retained their reputation after more than a decade in the business. Skip straight to the Kreuzberg site, a former metalwork and carpentry factory, with rattan panels and a jungle of greenery that cleverly break up the vast space. It has some serious co-working appeal, but of course the real draw is the coffee. This is the place to try (and buy) beans from Honduras, Ecuador and beyond. It's also branched out into a concise but lovely range of accessories that add panache to any breakfast bar. The perfect Sunday? Coffee at Bonanza and a visit to Kunstlerhaus Bethanien, a historic art gallery in a former 19th-century hospital.

Adalbertstrasse 70, 10999
Nearest station: Kottbusser Tor
bonanzacoffee.de

9

SOFI

A bakery on a slow food mission

SOFI blends ancient grains with a modern concept, using bread to spread the word about heritage farming practices that benefit both the environment and our health. How better to convince people than with cinnamon buns so good they nearly knock Zeit für Brot (no.27) off the top spot? Specialties range from sweet treats to pillowy loaves that incorporate the wild, spicy notes of emmer wheat and brioche-like champagne rye, all deftly wielded in the open-plan kitchen by a fleet of bakers. A tribute to Danish design, the space is filled with sleek lines, rustic ceramics and cosy wood, conjuring a Scandi-farmhouse-by-way-of-Mitte – spend an hour here and you'll expect to emerge into a rustling forest.

Sophienstrasse 21, 10178
Nearest station: Weinmeisterstrasse
sofiberlin.com

10

FELIX AUSTRIA

Traditional Austrian gasthaus

No trip to Berlin (or indeed Germany) is complete without schnitzel, though fact checkers will note the deep-fried, golden-crumbed veal or pork dish originally hails from Austria. Felix Austria still feels as Germanic it gets, with a wood-panelled ceiling and dark wood accents. On offer is a classic Austro-Germanic line-up: as well as schnitzel, you'll find *Spätzle* (glorious shredded noodles swimming in Emmental and *Bergkäse*, or mountain cheese) and *Kaiserschmarrn*, a deconstructed fluffy pancake scattered with rum-soaked raisins. Legendary Borchardt, beloved by 19th-century nobility and today's politicians, is another restaurant belonging to Berlin's schnitzel hall of fame, but Felix Austria gives it a run for its money – and has more wallet-friendly prices.

Bergmannstrasse 26, 10961
Nearest station: Gneisenaustrasse
felix-austria.eatbu.com

11

CAFÉ FRIEDA

All-day cafe and restaurant

You might not expect a conversation about one of Berlin's most-adored restaurants to revolve around a souped-up Mr Whippy, but the soft-serve at Café Frieda always gets a mention; the flavours are both numerous and unexpected, with purple sweet potato and yogurt swirl, a sumptuous forced rhubarb and milk number and a sunny mandarin gelato wreathed in shoestring strips of candied ginger. This alone should demonstrate the level of creativity at this farmer's market-supplied restaurant, where glowing orb lights hang low over the tabletops and music pulses from pale wood speakers. Whether you're after thick, squiggly udon noodles for lunch, mid-afternoon coffee or an evening aperitivo, Café Frieda will always knock it out of the park.

Lychener Strasse 37, 10437
Nearest station: Eberswalder Strasse
cafefrieda.de

12

OH, PANAMA

Inventive German cooking

Potsdammer Strasse's shop fronts read like a who's who of Berlin creatives – Andreas Murkudis (no.44), Galerie Thomas Fischer, Esther Schipper – and now sleek new kids on the block OH, PANAMA are no less. The third restaurant from Chef Ludwig Cramer-Klett of Katz Orange fame, it resides in a Mitte courtyard and delivers a menu of modern German cuisine. Blending together traditional and 'exotic' ideas in its ever-changing, ever-more-inventive menu, this is as far from schnitzel as you could get. A recent memorable hit was the 'sugar-loaf cabbage' – baked, pressed and grilled until caramelised, served with a molasses sauce

Potsdamer Strasse 91, 10785
Nearest station: Betriebsbahnhof Rummelsburg
oh-panama.com

13

MARKTHALLE NEUN

Celebration of regional German produce

This bustling market hall, which is as much a social event as it is a market, has a star-studded lineup of incredible meat from The Sausage Man Who Never Sleeps, bread from Domberger Brot-Werk and beautiful jars of spices at Soulspice. Once you're adequately stocked up with delicacies, grab a snack from one of the Markthalle restaurants – the *Buletten* (meatballs) from Baller's Place are a modern take on the Berliner classic – and take a seat at Monsieur Collard's wine bar. If you don't want to compete for service, the charismatic Collard has a second site on Lausitzer Platz, just a few minutes' walk away. It looks more like a cellar, but he puts tables outside where you can linger over champagne, crémant and plates of oysters.

Eisenbahnstrasse 42/43, 10997
Nearest station: Schlesisches Tor
markthalleneun.de

14

PAVILLON AM UFER

Superior sundowner location

Sundays are for *flanieren* (flaneuring), and Berlin's catwalk is the gravel path along Paul-Lincke-Ufer in Neukölln. The ultimate accessory? An Aperol spritz while sat under the lime trees at Pavillon am Ufer. This former currywurst *Büde* (food stand) has morphed into a cute and casual all-day cafe serving waffles, quiches and soups to the hungover masses. In summer, the outside-only space is ideal for Berlin's long evenings, perched right by Thielen-brücke, known as a top-notch spot for catching epic sunsets. Seating is limited and there are no toilets, but you can grab a sweet treat and strut along the canal with the rest of the fashionable flock.

Paul-Lincke-Ufer 4, 10999
Nearest station: Schönleinstrasse
instagram.com/pavillonamufer

15

KRAMER

Inventive and unpretentious wood-fire cooking

'Live-fire cooking' might sound like another over-hyped restaurant trend that leaves you rolling your eyes, but the food at Kramer is so flavoursome, it's won over even the most jaded cynics. Every dish from the globally inspired menu is excellently balanced, whether you're devouring sweet and zingy char-grilled pineapple ceviche served with aged tiger's milk (a Peruvian-style marinade made with lime juice), or the Iberico short ribs with sauerkraut-leaning cabbage. A short, sharp cocktail list is topped by a moreish mezcal sour, and the entire place smells strangely wonderful thanks to the aromas from the wood-burning fire.

Pannierstrasse 41, 12047
Nearest station: Schönleinstrasse
kramerberlin.com

16

GAZZO

Modern pizza with hyper-local ingredients

The advent of posh pizza has caused a stir in the city, and Berliners will debate their frontrunners as heatedly as they discuss their favourite clubs. One restaurant frequently topping the polls is Gazzo, and while the dispute for first place remains unresolved, Gazzo certainly wins hearts for its use of local produce – who knew you could get (genuinely great) burrata made in Brandenburg? Slices of salsiccia pizza and a dreamily creamy soft serve made with buffalo milk keep the Neukölln crowd queuing till late, even on a Sunday. If you're not willing to wait, Salami Social Club and Falco Slice are similarly delicious but with smaller queues.

Hobrechtstrasse 57, 12047
Nearest station: Schönleinstrasse
de.gazzopizza.com

17

BARRA

Exquisite small plates from an acclaimed kitchen

Low lighting, open-plan kitchen, a single oyster served on a bed of pebbles: Barra bears all the hallmarks of the modern natural wine bistro. Though on the fancier end of the restaurant spectrum, it's worth it to experience head chef Daniel Remers' incredible eye for simple yet striking flavours – but prepare for the bill to be pushed up by an all-too inviting wine list dominated by dry, cider-like pet nats and gluggable orange wines. Finish with a vibe shift and a large, frothy pils at O Tannenbaum on Hermannstrasse, where glittery streamers more than compensate for the lack of swanky hand soap.

Okerstrasse 2, 12049
Nearest station: Leinestrasse
barraberlin.com

18

OTTO

Effortless brilliance and show-stopping ingredients

On the face of it, Otto might seem like yet another natural wine and small plates restaurant, packaged up with concrete walls and raw metal counters. But within this light-filled Oderberger Strasse space you'll find both style and substance. Chef-patron Vadim Otto Ursus lovingly creates menus inspired by regionally sourced produce, leaning on his experience under René Redzepi and other internationally acclaimed chefs. As a child, Ursus' family had a *Dacha* (wood cabin) near Berlin, where the chef learned to forage; the same plot of land is today home to Otto's test kitchen and garden, where the team experiment to create dishes like powder-pink rhubarb sorbet drizzled with sour cherry blossom oil and a splash of Lambrusco, or lamb belly croquettes with anchovy mayo.

Oderberger Strasse 56, 10435
Nearest station: Eberswalder Strasse
otto-berlin.net

19
ST. BART

Elevated pub-style fare with a cult Sunday roast

St. Bart describes itself as a British gastropub, which, if you're English, doesn't actually do this Gräfekiez hero justice. The food does have a few pub-style influences: there are Scotch eggs, pies and even a Sunday roast, but the dishes have a dash of small-plate elegance that elevates the whole dining experience. The menu is a perfect balance of deliciousness and creativity, with artful plates of golden chanterelle mushrooms, bacon and a whole egg yolk, chicory caesar salad and nduja panzanella. The cocktail menu is just as bold, offering frothy, punchy pink rhubarb sours and the dirtiest martinis, while the wine list is dominated by natural, low-intervention varieties. If this is a gastropub, it's the modern, Berlin version.

Gräfestrasse 71, 10967
Nearest station: Schönleinstrasse
stbartpub.com

20

JAJA WEIN

Pared-back natural wine bistro

One of the first bistros in Berlin to do natural wines and seasonal small plates, JAJA is a bit of an institution, so prepare to see and be seen by Neukölln locals with slicked-back hair, enormous trousers and tiny handbags. Delicious (and mostly German) wines are served with classic Berliner attitude – meaning copious knowledge but not quite as much enthusiasm – under the gaze of JAJA's light-sculpture mascot, a neon-pink ghost clutching a wine glass. All the food is organic and locally sourced – look out for the delicate Hamachi tuna crudo and the trio of tiny pork dishes, with slices of meat and a caramelised rib served with plum sauce, pork-filled *Maultaschen* (German ravioli) and soft, juicy leeks.

Weichselstrasse 7, 12043
Nearest station: Rathaus Neukölln
jajawein.de

21

HALLMANN & KLEE

Daring Michelin-starred dining

The skill of Sarah Hallmann's all-women kitchen was finally recognised with a Michelin star in 2024. It was a landmark shift for Berlin, where fine dining is usually equated with stiff white tablecloths and stiffer service. The delicate, German-accented tasting menu is the talk of the town, thanks to dishes like wafer-thin slices of custard-yellow kohlrabi marinated in mandarin juice with a lick of raw chilli, steak tartare that's been given a modern spin with wagyu beef and crunchy Jerusalem artichoke crisps and chubby, hand-rolled pici noodles laden with umami from black nori powder and yuzu lime. It's nigh on impossible getting a reservation and the menu will set you back a pretty penny, but their beautiful plates will be a meal to remember.

Böhmische Strasse 13, 12055
Nearest station: Sonnenallee
hallmann-klee.de

22

ESTELLE

Modern European small plates and pizza

Estelle identifies as a neighbourhood restaurant, and it's immediately clear the neighbourhood in question is Prenzlauer Berg. Natural wines? Tick. Scandi chairs? Tick. Pickled vegetables displayed in decorative jars? *Tick*. Clichés aside, Estelle is a restaurant you *do* actually want nearby, with a crowd-pleasing menu including superb pan-fried oyster mushrooms on spelt atop a tantalising swoop of white bean sauce. Feeling more low-key? They're also known for their pizzas, all chewiness and charred blisters, with inventive toppings like pickled, caramelised and roasted onion. The soups and Caesar salad at lunch provide the perfect counterpart to Estelle's signature oil-soaked focaccia, served with a big daub of caramelised onion butter.

Kopenhagener Strasse 12a, 10437
Nearest station: Schönhauser Allee
estelle-dining.com

23

OMONI

Hidden sushi spot in sleek surrounds

Omoni's exterior is so discrete that some customers try to enter the apartment next door – making it all the more surprising when you walk into a buzzy, wood-panelled restaurant stretching far to the back. The best seat in the house is at the counter overlooking the sushi kitchen, where the bespectacled chef is known to slowly make his way through a bottle of excellent red while he precisely slices and dices some of Berlin's best sushi. If you're feeling a bit overwhelmed by the extensive variations of maki and sashimi on offer, the two-person Kopenhagener menu offers such delectable triangles of seared tuna coated in sesame seeds and strips of salmon belly that you could easily polish off the entire thing solo.

Kopenhagener Strasse 14, 10437
Nearest station: Schönhauser Allee
instagram.com/omoniberlin

24

SATHUTU

Vivid homage to Sri Lankan cooking

Sathutu's minimalist white space on Rykestrasse sets the scene for bold, vibrantly hued Sri Lankan-inspired cooking. Fragrant black dhal is served with puffy paratha and a scoop of burnt butter; paneer comes in a sunshine-yellow sauce and a sprinkling of crunchy toasted grains; and jaw-droppingly good tuna crudo sits resplendent in a bath of salted lime and coconut milk so delicious you could slurp it straight from the bowl. The drinks menu is no slouch, either, with serves like silky mango lassi turbocharged with a slug of bourbon. Fastidious Prenzlauer Berg locals will point out the lack of vegan options, but Sathutu is fire from start to finish – and the kitchen *can* actually whip up vegan versions of almost all dishes.

Rykestrasse 15, 10405
Nearest station: Senefelderplatz
sathutu.berlin

25

LA BOLOGNINA

Perfect plates of pasta with a vinyl soundtrack

Pillows of pistachio- and mortadella-stuffed ravioli; strozzapreti coated in grass-green pesto; triangoli packed with potato and served with shavings of lemon zest – the rotating pasta menu at intimate Italian restaurant La Bolognina is good enough to make even a seasoned nonna sit up and take notice. The man behind this beloved Neukölln spot is Luca Spinogatti, who also DJs under the alias The Ivory Boy, so the plates of perfect pasta are complemented by a genre-defying vinyl playlist and, while the restaurant is tiny, the negronis are anything but.

Donaustrasse 107, 12043
Nearest station: Rathaus Neukölln
labolognina.de

26

ITA BISTRO

Fusion food centred around a wood-fired oven

With a bold menu that salutes South and Central American cuisine, Ita Bistro breaks away from the small plates crowd. The fearless verve is down to owners Micaela Longo (the Argentinian-born, Mexico-raised sommelier) and Javier Barbosa (the Colombian head chef) who wanted to create a restaurant that defies labels. The proof is in the pudding, and Ita's savoury but densely creamy asparagus ice cream, served with dulce de leche, is a creative triumph, as are the eye-catching tetelas or spiced potatoes topped with hispi cabbage, seawood mayonnaise and shiso leaf, while the celeriac-rubbed pork chop served on a slick of bright red mojo sauce brings you straight to the Canary Islands. It's bad manners not to greet the T-Rex toilet roll holder in the bathroom.

Lettestrasse 9, 10437
Nearest station: Eberswalder Strasse
ita-berlin.de

27

ZEIT FÜR BROT

Organic bakery famous for cinnamon rolls

Zeit Für Brot's *Zimtschecke* (cinnamon roll) has attained something of a celebrity status in Berlin's pastry circles and, when you sample these plump, pillowy delights, you'll understand why. So popular is the *Schnecke* that the group have gone on to create souped-up versions of their classic, among which the walnut variety is particularly good and the apple is a close second. In a nod to the German enthusiasm for seasonal eating, at certain times of year a rhubarb *Schnecke* is also available – but these sell out almost immediately. On Sundays, when all other shops are closed, the bakeries become a bit of a social hub, with queues that snake around the block and not a crumb left on the shelves by closing time.

Alte Schönhauser Strasse 4, 10119
Nearest station: Rosa-Luxemburg-Platz
Other locations: Prenzlauer Berg, Charlottenburg, Mitte,
Wilmersdorf
zeitfuerbrot.com

28

BANH MI STABLE

Sell-out Vietnamese sandwiches

During the 1980s, an influx of Vietnamese migrants seeking work in East Germany and refugees fleeing the Vietnam War to West Berlin led to both halves of the city boasting a thriving Vietnamese community – and a wealth of excellent Vietnamese restaurants. You'll find noodle joints hidden around almost every corner, but recent years have also seen a slew of bánh mì shops open their doors. One of the best is Banh Mi Stable, near Rosa-Luxemburg-Platz, slinging sandwiches to long lines of devoted fans. Small, baguette-style rice flour bread is stuffed to bursting with crispy pork, chicken or tofu, then piled high with vegetables and fresh herbs. Once they're gone, they're gone, so make sure to come early.

Alte Schönhauser Strasse 50, 10119
Nearest station: Rosa-Luxemburg-Platz
instagram.com/banhmistable

29

ORANGERIE
NEUKÖLLN

Comely cafe and bar with a capacious terrace

Orangerie is a beautiful all-day dining space in a beautiful neighbourhood, accessed by Hermannstrasse, one of Berlin's least beautiful stations. No matter; head straight to the immaculately landscaped Körnerpark to find this stunning, secret-feeling spot, all six-metre-high ceilings, enormous windows and velvet banquettes. It's open during the day for coffee, cake and a fleeting seasonal lunch menu served for just two hours. If you miss out, there are still miso sours, habanero margaritas and plentiful regular parties to enjoy, not to mention the spacious terrace that screams 'spritz'. There's a neighbouring gallery, too, Galerie im Körnerpark, so between that and the vegan antipasti, you've got your afternoon sorted.

Schierker Strasse 8, 12051
Nearest station: Hermannstrasse
orangerie-nk.de

30

HARD WAX

Hallowed record store and legendary label

Hard Wax has been a temple for techno, dub and reggae devotees for more than 30 years, acting as a key player during techno's 1990s boom. Recently forced to swap their Paul-Lincke-Ufer location for the former power plant Kraftwerk, they're now fittingly rubbing shoulders with legendary clubs Tresor and OHM (no.88). If you discount the dub booming from the speakers, the new space has studious library undertones, thanks to the quiet reverence of both staff and clientele. Flick through rows of records, each sleeve marked with descriptive signposting like 'funky aquatic techno', 'gloomy, dramatic drone-tinged album' and 'noisy, puristic banger', or take the vinyls out for a spin at the sound booths.

Köpenicker Strasse 70, 10179
Nearest station: Heinrich-Heine-Strasse
hardwax.com

31

SHAKESPEARE & SONS

Indie English bookstore and bagel shop

Even if you're not a bookworm, the scent of freshly baked pastries and bagels will lure you to Shakespeare & Sons on Warschauer Strasse. This beloved bookstore has an excellent array of new and secondhand English-language books lining its wooden shelves, a roster of regular book launches, author readings and writing workshops. The jewel in the crown? The on-site sister company, Fine Bagel Co. Bookend an afternoon of browsing with a pit stop in the cafe, where you'll find glossy New York-style bagels with an irresistibly dense crumb. No matter whether you're eating the pastrami-packed 'everything' bagel or the lox slathered with homemade schmear, you definitely won't be leaving hungry.

Warschauer Strasse 74, 10243
Nearest station: Frankfurter Tor
shakespeareandsons.com

32

DO YOU READ ME?!

Indie gem celebrating all things print

They say print is dead, but it's truly alive and kicking at independent store do you read me?!, dedicated to the kind of lust-worthy selection of glossy magazines, bound screenplays and unusual books that die-hard collectors dream of. Founded by Mark Kiessling as a creative venture beyond his own design practice, there's an unsurprising focus on art and design in almost every language, but you'll find topics like feminism and AI celebrated here, too. The store sits beside galleries and boutiques on the quietly historic Auguststrasse; don't leave Mitte without exploring the streets, maybe stopping at Hackbarth's (no.80) brass bar for a glass of Riesling.

Auguststrasse 28, 10117
Nearest station: Rosenthaler Platz
doyoureadme.de

33

R.S.V.P. PAPIER

Aladdin's cave of colourful stationery and paper

The U-Bahn stations of Weinmeisterstrasse, Rosenthaler Platz and Rosa-Luxemburg-Platz in Mitte form a three-cornered area with an effect comparable to the infamous Bermuda Triangle. But it won't be you disappearing – it'll be your money, swiftly traded for gorgeous knick-knacks from independent, design-led boutiques. Chief offender is stationery and paper shop R.S.V.P., where you'll find a vibrant array of printed goods patterned with everything from psychedelic marbling to graphic sketches of people doing yoga. Beautiful greeting cards (a rarity in Berlin), pens, pencils, notebooks and sketchpads will make hearts sing. There's more temptation around the corner, with tea shop Paper & Tea, Le Labo, EcoAlf and so many more. See? Dangerous.

Mulackstrasse 26, 10119
Nearest station: Weinmeisterstrasse
rsvp-berlin.de

34

MODULOR

Multi-floored haven of creative supplies

With its winding maze of channels between neatly stacked piles of creative supplies, Modulor is evocative of a certain Swedish home store – but this time, for arts and crafts. This one-stop shop is a cornucopia of DIY supplies, with air-dry clay, sheets of MDF, a huge tool section and a rainbow of the folding plastic storage baskets by Aykasa that are ubiquitous to every Berlin home. If you're looking for a break from the Saturday crowds, head to the hushed, mid-century-inspired furniture shop on the first floor or take a seat at the coffee bar sandwiched into Modulor's shared entrance with neighbouring bookshop Buchhandlung Moritzplatz.

Prinzenstrasse 85, 10969
Nearest station: Moritzplatz
modulor.de

35

KADEWE

Retail institution and a supreme food hall

Often likened to Harrods, KaDeWe is *the* place to go for high-end shopping in Berlin – but its appeal lies in far more than clothes. Zoom up to the top floor by lift and emerge into the labyrinthine Food Hall, where you'll find posh food shopping (think Kobe beef and intricate petit fours) and a selection of bars and restaurants offering the crème de la crème of the city's drinking and dining. For all of Berlin's trendy bistros hawking oysters, KaDeWe is still the best place to eat them, while the bottle-lined corner known as the Champagner Bar is a must for its seemingly endless selection of fizz, silver service from waistcoat-wearing waiters and Olympic-level people watching.

Tauentzienstrasse 21–24, 10789
Nearest station: Wittenbergplatz
kadewe.de

36

HUMANA
FRANKFURTER ALLEE

Secondhand outfitter of Berlin

Walk past Frankfurter Tor U-Bahn station on a Tuesday morning and you'll see a line of stylish individuals waiting outside a set of double doors. No, this isn't a hot new club; it's the entrance to the flagship site of charity shop group Humana, on the day they do their weekly restock. Occupying a former department store, the Frankfurter Tor site's enormous windows, high ceilings and marble stair-case result in a peculiar mismatch with the scent of moth balls as you paw your way through racks of puffer coats, fisherman's jackets and an astonishing profusion of jeans, all on sale for as little as €4. You'll find all kinds of weird and wonderful items, whether you're more into purple satin-lined Paul Smith blazers or, er, crotchless denim chaps.

Frankfurter Tor 3, 10243
Nearest station: Frankfurter Tor
humana-second-hand.de

37

MAISINGER

Beautiful boutique with pan-global wares

Anyone who doesn't want to be tempted by an array of design-forward accessories and home-wares should look away now, because this shop is filled to the rafters (or at least the high Berlin ceiling) with trinkets picked out by owner Krista Elfinger. The shelves burst with colour: boldly hued felt coasters, a rainbow of candles in all shapes and sizes, flourescent pink tassels and hand-painted crockery, while in a blue room at the back, you'll find larger pieces like quilts and cushions, all testament to Elfinger's impeccable taste. Her eye stems from a background in fashion design and a nouse for curation: she's persuaded craftsmen all over the world to sell via her Berlin boutique, so purchases here are often one of a kind.

Veteranenstrasse 22, 10119
Nearest station: Rosenthaler Platz
maisinger.com

38

VOO STORE

Minimalist concept shop and events space

Tucked away in a pistachio-tiled Kreuzberg *Hinter-hof* (courtyard), Voo Store is probably Berlin's most famous concept shop. Concrete walls set the scene for a smorgasbord of micro fringes, ugly-chic trainers and designer goods to covet – a far cry from the location's past life as a locksmith's. Alongside a selection of very small items of clothing for very large prices, the store is also home to an exhibition area, Voo Space, where it partners with brands like Converse or Clarks (yes, the classic British shoemaker), and a charity market in aid of international art project Operndorf Arika. Within its walls you'll also find on-site cafe Toki where you can buy bottles of the sensationally popular ruby-red Lambrusco Frauen Power (Women Power).

Oranienstrasse 24, 10999
Nearest station: Kottbusser Tor
voostore.com

39
HALLESCHES HAUS

Cute co-working cafe and tantalising store

You could (and should) spend a whole day at Hallesches Haus, the shop and cafe situated in a listed canal-side building in Kreuzberg. High ceilings, abundant greenery and plenty of natural light attract a horde of co-workers during the week. If you need a moment of distraction, spot the faces sweetly sketched into the broken tiles and grouting. Don't leave without exploring the gorgeous on-site shop, where you'll find covetable design items to yearn over, including billowing pink, Mr. Whippy-shaped lamps and three-dimensional laser-cut vases in a kaleidoscope of brilliant colours.

Tempelhofer Ufer 1, 10961
Nearest station: Hallesches Tor
hallescheshaus.com

40

THE GOOD STORE

Curated contemporary vintage

Square-toed strappy sandals from Miista, semi-precious ear cuffs by Munich-based jewellery designer Saskia Diez, a grass-green ruched leather Prada handbag: if you were sentenced to only dress in clothes from one shop for the rest of your life, The Good Store would be your best choice. This Neukölln stalwart is the kind of secondhand heaven sartorialists dream of, with a careful curation of vintage designer treasures, fine jewellery and other essentials, covering a real spectrum of labels and prices. Rumour has it you can try negotiating on cost and the impeccably sleek sales staff may choose to make a whispered call to the owner...

Pannierstrasse 31, 12047
Nearest station: Hermannplatz
thegoodstore.berlin

41
STANDERT BICYCLES

Berlin-made bikes and coffee

Working as a part-time bike courier to fund his studies in industrial design, founder Max von Senger was looking for a set of wheels that could do it all: sturdy enough to survive the city's infamous cobbled streets but sleek enough to hold its own on longer rides. His answer was to design his own frame in steel, which became Standert's signature – that, and the brand's pleasingly colourful signature material. The brand's new Friedrichstrasse site displays more performance-focused frames and matching gear within its huge wood and glass storefront, high ceilings and concrete walls. There's also a small cafe inside where you can talk shop and drink coffee from local roastery Tres Cabezas. It's fair to say that this is a cycling über-brand that's anything but standard.

Friedrichstrasse 23a, 10969
Nearest station: Kochstrasse
standert.de

42

OCELOT

Multilingual bookshop and cafe

Ocelot describes itself as 'not just another bookstore', and for once this line actually rings true. You'll find heaps of bestsellers and bright covers, laid flat in an dizzying patchwork rainbow, but look closer and there's more than meets the eye. While lots of the books are in German, there's also a healthy English section and, crucially, an array of picture books in Arabic and other languages – a rare boon for the city. An in-store cafe elevates Ocelot to the perfect afternoon pit stop. If you'd rather be outside, bring your new treasures across the road to the suntrap of Weinberg Park, with gently elevated slopes allowing for prime Prenzlauer Berg people-watching.

Brunnenstrasse 181, 10119
Nearest station: Rosenthaler Platz
instagram.com/ocelotberlin

43

BILDBAND

Photography store/creative community hub

Contemporary photography bookshop Bildband holds a mix of titles documenting Berlin's history, collectors' editions from big names like Martin Parr and self-published titles by independent creatives. Co-founded by former photojournalist Joe Dilworth and Thomas Ernst, it's also a photographers' hub with a hopping social calendar of talks and book launches, a community dark room and workshops with artists like the incredible bookmaker Tomasz Laczny. It's easy whiling away an afternoon here, immersing yourself in the collection; when you're done, amble past the Wassterturm, a folly-come-water tower ideal for sunset views, closing the day with the city's finest tasting menu at Otto (no.18) on Oderberger Strasse.

Immanuelkirchstrasse 33, 10405
Nearest station: Senefelderplatz
bildbandberlin.com

44

ANDREAS MURKUDIS

Iconic homewares and fashion

You can't talk about fashion or design in Berlin without mentioning Andreas Murkudis and his revered stores in Mitte – equal parts retail heaven and tourist attraction for the creatively inclined. Over 20 years and four shop openings, the GDR-born Berlin icon has shaped the city's taste in everything from porcelain to sandals, and his flagship is a must-see. Formerly home to the Tagesspiegel newspaper printing press, wares are laid out like precious artefacts in the vast space, a wink at Murkudis' previous role as director of the Museum der Dinge (the Museum of Things). Over the road, visit Andreas Murkudis 98, which has been turned into a fully-furnished proto-apartment, so you can live out your design fantasies – if only for a few minutes.

Potsdamer Strasse 81, 10785
Nearest station: Kurfürstenstrasse
andreasmurkudis.com

45

MARTIN-GROPIUS-BAU

Sprawling neo-Renaissance landmark

Yayoi Kusama and Frida Kahlo are among the luminaries whose works have graced the grand halls of the Gropius Bau, one of Berlin's best galleries and cultural epicentre. The building itself reflects Berlin's history: originally constructed in the 1800s by Martin Gropius (great uncle to Bauhaus founder Walter Gropius), it was partially destroyed during World War II and retains its injuries, immortalised in bullet holes that mark the external walls. Gropius Bau hosts more than just art: it's also a space for music events including the city's annual Jazz Festival. At its heart is a central courtyard which forms its own immersive (and highly Instagrammable) exhibition space. Don't miss Beba, the Jewish-influenced restaurant with beautiful salads, breads and a banging Sunday brunch.

Niederkirchnerstrasse 7, 10963
Nearest station: Potsdamer Platz
berlinerfestspiele.de

46

FOTOGRAFISKA

Fresh photography meets culinary flair

There are many reasons to visit Fotografiska: its collection of world-class photography, for instance; or being able to swan around with a glass of *Sekt* (German sparkling wine) and the excellent selection of dining options. Can you name another gallery with its own on-site bakery? Displaying its works like carefully illuminated jewels in the dim hallways of Mitte's historic Tacheles building, the former squat still bears graffiti from the artist collective that occupied it. There's always something here to capture the imagination – in addition to a rotating exhibition schedule, screenings and panel discussions also take place on topics from video games to sustainability and pyschedelics.

Oranienburger Strasse 54, 10117
Nearest station: Oranienburger Tor
berlin.fotografiska.com

47

HAUS DER KULTUREN DER WELT

Culturally eye-opening curation

Venture beyond the government buildings and green spaces of Tiergarten and you'll discover former congress hall Haus der Kulturen der Welt. House of World Cultures, or HKW for short, hosts a roster of exhibitions, concerts and dance performances that platform marginalised communities outside the standard European lens. Whatever you come see, exhibitions are sensitively curated – just be sure to pick up a pamphlet before visiting, as otherwise you may need some help figuring out quite what you're looking at. In a city famous for its sense of freedom, HKW feels like a key part of Berlin's open-minded attitude.

John-Foster-Dulles-Allee 10, 10557
Nearest station: Bundestag
hkw.de

48

BERLINISCHE GALERIE

Distinctive gallery celebrating Berlin-made art

The clue is in the name: instead of focusing on any single style or period, the Berlinische Galerie displays only artworks that were made here in the city. It's a must-see for anyone enamoured with Berlin's creative spirit. You'll find everything from exhibitions of Edvard Munch's Berlin-originated work to a section devoted entirely to Dadaism. Among the paintings and sculptures, touchable renderings of the most significant works make things more inclusive for the visually impaired. Around the corner from the gallery, Modulor (no.34) is Berlin's one-stop-shop for creative supplies, and brunch spot Frühstück 3000 serves mad fusion takes on breakfast favourites (think kimchi croissants) alongside pleasingly bone-dry sparkling wine.

Alte Jakobstrasse 124–128, 10969
Nearest station: Kochstrasse
berlinischegalerie.de

49

KW INSTITUTE FOR CONTEMPORARY ART

Unpacking complex themes in a Mitte courtyard

Opened in a former margarine factory in Mitte in the 1990s, KW prides itself on more than aesthetics. Be it on techno or the digital economy, every exhibition is designed to spark conversations around modern topics. Today, singular exhibitions neatly span the multi-storeyed space and are bolstered by a packed calendar of events from deep dives into archival material to conversations on self and habitat. KW aims to challenge, and it's 50/50 whether you leave feeling enriched or confused. Never fear – if you need a minute to digest, have a breather (and an Aperol spritz) at Bravo, the Italian restaurant and cafe in the sun-dappled *Hof* (courtyard) downstairs.

Auguststrasse 69, 10117
Nearest stations: Weinmeisterstrasse,
Oranienburger Strasse
kw-berlin.de

50
C/O

Celebration of photography and the visual arts

Berlin's art scene is renowned for being politically vocal, in part due to a history that saw art and culture abused for propaganda purposes. To find the best of it, you'll need to go beyond the main heavy hitters like the Nationalgalerie, to independent institutions that have maintained a political edge and boast cult followings for their curation. One of these is non-profit foundation C/O, just off Tiergarten, with interiors offering a mid-century throwback: concrete columns, boxy open ceilings and flagged-stone floors. The exhibitions are hard-hitting and socially relevant: past highlights include a retrospective from performance artist Valie Export and a powerfully moving exposition of rape and institutional failure by Laia Abril.

Hardenbergstrasse 22–24, 10623
Nearest station: Kurfürstendamm
co-berlin.org/en

Swarovski Book of Dreams Volume II, 2015

51

NEUE NATIONALGALERIE

Sleek structure housing 20th-century art

While there are plenty of modern treasures within its walls, the most impressive part of the Neue Nationalgalerie may be the building itself. Ludwig Mies van der Rohe's 1960s glass-and-steel structure, hunkered down on a raised concrete platform, is a design statement: on entering, you'll encounter a completely bare space, all long, dappled shadows and hushed, echoing tones. The works are tucked away underground, where you'll discover long white-walled hallways displaying Dalí and Gerhard Richter, as well as a bust of legendary Käthe Kollwitz, the first female artist to become a professor at the Prussian Academy of Arts in 1919.

Potsdamer Strasse 50, 10785
Nearest station: Potsdamer Platz
smb.museum/en/museums-institutions/
neue-nationalgalerie

52

BERLINER PHILHARMONIE

Legendary music hall

This sprawling building, evoking a brick-and-mortar marquee, is the permanent home of the Berliner Philharmoniker. Beyond classical music, the concert hall is famous for an experimental programme that makes space for events like Strom, a two-day festival devoted to electronic music that previously saw German musician Robert Henke deliver a jaw-dropping audiovisual performance by programming five early computers. The Phil has had a trickle-down effect on venues around the city, like quirky Piano Salon Christophori in Wedding, where walls decorated with the innards of old broken-down classical pianos and chandeliers give the space as much atmosphere as the fiercely engaged audience.

Herbert-von-Karajan-Strasse 1, 10785
Nearest station: Potsdamer Platz
berliner-philharmoniker.de

53

REICHSTAG

Architectural and historical icon

The home of the German parliament is a symbol of democracy, a monument to the past and an architectural marvel. It's seen a lot in its time: almost burnt to the ground in 1933 during the Nazi's rise to power, bombed to bits in World War II and then wrapped in fabric and turned into a work of art by Christo and Jean-Claude in 1995. Spot its dazzling dome from afar, added in 1999 as a reinvention of the original steel and glass cupola that dominated its silhouette when it was first built in 1884. Take a free tour of the Reichstag or book breakfast on the roof at Käfer, with access to the dome's spiralling walkway alongside your smoked salmon and prosecco.

Platz der Republik 1, 11011
Nearest station: Bundestag
bundestag.de

54

DARK MATTER

Trippy immersive light art exhibition

This light-art exhibition in a blacked-out Lichtenberg factory is as Berlin as they come, with seven separate spaces of partially interactive audiovisual displays. Light artist Christopher Bauder and his studio WHITEvoid are the brains behind the operation, also responsible for installations like SKALAR, the travelling exhibition using kinetic mirrors, roving lights and a multi-channel sound system. But where SKALAR is meant to be watched, DARK MATTER invites participation. It certainly makes for an unforgettable experience (going hungover is very much not recommended) and its mystery is part of the fun. The unique three-dimensional sound system will get audiophiles going – if it whets your appetite for a dance, super-club Sisyphos is just down the road.

Köpenicker Chaussee 46, 10317
Nearest station: Betriebsbahnhof Rummelsburg
darkmatter.berlin

55

HAMBURGER BAHNHOF

Modern art in striking surrounds

Railway terminus to cultural hub could well be one of the best makeovers a train station has ever received. Ample light and high ceilings afford a unique canvas for bold structural pieces, like Eva Fabregas' recent installation, *Devouring Lovers* that saw the main hall filled with gently vibrating pink, red and purple forms evocative of body parts. Their permanent collection is filled with well-known pieces from the modern art roster including Warhol and Lichtenstein, but also more radical work by Joseph Beuys, whose massive tallow fat sculptures embedded with millivoltmeters reside in their own temperature-controlled room.

Invalidenstrasse 50, 10557
Nearest station: Berlin Hauptbahnhof
smb.museum/en/museums-institutions/
hamburger-bahnhof

56

JÜDISCHES MUSEUM

Powerful exploration of Jewish history

This enormous maze of a museum sensitively and comprehensively covers Jewish history in Germany, which means you'll need several hours to do it justice. The core exhibition is undoubtedly the main draw, occupying the old Prussian Court of Justice and a titanium-zinc-fronted structure designed by Daniel Libeskind in 2001. The exceptional building is filled with unique design accents, starting with sloping underground pathways that lead you into the Holocaust Tower, a silent, grey chamber that feels like a literal dead end. But make time for the special exhibitions to see the Jüdisches Museum flex its curatorial skill. The recent, punchily named *Sex: Jewish Position*s was a landmark show, kick-starting conversations around sex in art and film within Jewish society.

Lindenstrasse 9–14, 10969
Nearest station: Hallesches Tor
jmberlin.de

57

KÖNIG GALERIE

Private gallery in a 1960s Brutalist church

Contemporary artworks take on near-holy status at König Galerie, which occupies a reimagined church in Mitte. Cavernous ceilings, clean lines and spaciously laid out concrete inspire quiet contemplation and reverence for gallerists Lena and Johann König's roster of young, international, interdisciplinary artists. When daylight floods through the two high windows, intricate shadows play out on the floors of the 20-metre-high gallery. The contrast between the pared-back architecture and the delicate, colourful exhibitions make for an alluring juxtaposition – particularly the giant, textured green gherkin sculpture, most recently displayed at the centre of the winding concrete staircase.

Alexandrinenstrasse 118–121, 10969
Nearest station: Prinzenstrasse
koeniggalerie.com

58

KINDL CENTRE FOR CONTEMPORARY ART

Arts space in a former brewery

The German obsession with beer needs no intro-
duction – name another country with such strict
brewing quality laws – and it'll come as no surprise
that the most historic breweries once occupied
spaces that feel more akin to palaces. Case in point:
the former Kindl brewery in Neukölln. These days,
the boiler room and old powerhouse are home to a
collection of contemporary art, with curators max-
imizing space in this enormous structure through
site-specific works such as Roman Signer's yellow
aircraft, hung upside down from the 20-metre-high
ceiling in 2016. Hopheads won't be disappointed
either, as you can still see the six copper kettles, once
the largest brewing pans in Europe, and enjoy beer
brewed on-site by independent brewers Rollberg.

Am Sudhaus 3, 12053
Nearest station: Rathaus Neukölln
kindl-berlin.de

59

BOROS FOUNDATION

Private collection housed in a behemoth bunker

This megalithic concrete building on Reinhardt-strasse has undergone almost as many reinventions as Berlin itself: originally a Nazi bunker, it went on to become a Soviet prison and then a night club before housing the private art collection of patrons Christian and Karen Boros, who themselves live in a glass atrium on the building's roof. Pass through the metre-thick walls to gawp at how they've reimagined the raw concrete corridors and rooms, making way for immersive installations like a colossal tree by Ai Weiwei that required the removal of an entire floor, or a popcorn machine that ran unsupervised for years. The gallery is only accessible by private tour and you'll need to book at least a month in advance, but it's worth the wait.

Reinhardtstrasse 20, 10117
Nearest station: Oranienburger Tor
sammlung-boros.de

60

VOLKSBÜHNE

Storied theatre with a radical programme

Contrary to its forward-thinking arts programme, the Volksbühne's brown carpets, brown marble and wood-panelled walls are a time machine straight back to the GDR. Skip the bars by the entrance and instead head down to Kantine, accessed by a semi-secret door to the right of the main stage, to find a lino-floored canteen serving *Bier vom Fass* (on tap) and Aperol spritz. You can eat here and, if you time your visit after a show, you may be treated to some surreal scenes – most recently, older German theatre-goers (and even a few cast members) enjoying their freshly poured pils to the soundtrack of *The Piña Colada Song*.

Linienstrasse 227, 10178
Nearest station: Rosa-Luxemburg-Platz
volksbuehne.berlin

61

PFAUENINSEL

King's folly-turned-summer hideaway

With a turreted fairytale castle, free-roaming sheep, horses, peacocks and, erm, racoons, Pfaueninsel feels like a playground for grown-ups – and that's precisely what it was (or what it was designed for). In the late 18th century, King Frederick William II made the island into a lovers' hideaway to share with his favourite mistress. It was later turned into a menagerie housing everything from wolves to crocodiles, all of which were eventually moved into what is now the Berlin Zoo – apart from the peacocks, whose descendants today strut around Pfaueninsel's manicured gardens as regally as the king himself. At the island's heart, you'll find a cafe that, if not quite fit for royalty, is certainly fit for the German afternoon ritual of *Kaffee und Kuchen* (coffee and cake).

Pfaueninsel, 14109
Nearest station: Wannsee

62

TEGELER SEE

Berlin's Riviera

With its glittering water, elegant sailboats and sandy coves, Tegeler See feels worlds away from Tempelhof and Checkpoint Charlie, but it's actually just further along the same U-Bahn line. The lake is vast and sprinkled with islands, and when the entire city is desperate to escape Berlin's 35-degree summers by getting into the nearest body of water, Tegeler See is big enough to swallow the crowds and leave no crumbs, so you won't need to get there early and put down a towel (the Germans always win that game anyway). The path along the water's edge also makes for a good long stroll through and there's many a simple *Imbiss* (casual food stop) to keep you fuelled.

Reinickendorf, 13505
Nearest station: Tegel

63
KRUMME LANKE

Canopied oasis

Berlin is a city made up of 3,000 lakes, of which Krumme Lanke, located at the end of the U3 U-Bahn, is certainly one of the most idyllic: a short walk from the station brings you to a stretch of water surrounded by sand and swaying willows. The main path will land you at the FKK beach (that's *Freikörperkultur*, or free body culture – a deeply ingrained German movement promoting the health benefits of being naked in the open air). If that sounds a bit overwhelming, keep walking and you'll find fully clothed stretches. After a dip, make your way to Schlachtensee, the next lake down, to visit the Fischerhütte for the quintessentially German summertime-favourite: *Wurstsalat* (sausage salad).

Krumme Lanke, 14163
Nearest station: Krumme Lanke

64

MAUERPARK

Iconic flea market and social hub

Berlin's most beautiful green space this is not, but that hasn't stopped Mauerpark from becoming a point of focus for the community. It comes into its own on Sundays, when the anaemic-looking grass thrums with flea market devotees and a roster of buskers perform everything from stirring Adele covers to cacophonous electronic noise. You'll undoubtedly encounter the drum circle where, rain or shine, fully clothed or topless, a group plays with mesmeric ferocity. Grab an Augustiner helles beer from the *Späti* (corner shop) and play Berlin-bingo as you spot techno heads, crusties and more mullets than you can shake a wurst at. If it's real vintage finds you are after, head to nearby Arkonaplatz for higher-quality (and higher-priced) treasures.

Bernauer Strasse 63, 13355
Nearest station: Eberswalder Strasse

65

TEMPELHOFER FELD

Fiery sunsets in historic surrounds

There's nothing quite as magical as a summer evening on Tempelhofer Feld, when the grassy expanse floods with golden light, imbuing even the smallest interaction with drama and romance. The silhouette of the old airport building and runways give a real sense of place, offering a very tangible demonstration of Berlin's ability to adapt (see also its community gardens and accommodation for refugees in disused hangars). Bringing pizza and *Späti*-purchased helles to watch the roller skaters and kite boarders is a right of passage, and on sunny days the Feld often has spontaneous open airs – informal day parties that reflect the city's dance-loving spirit.

Tempelhofer Damm, 12101
Nearest station: Tempelhof

66

WINTERFELDTPLATZ MARKT

Atmospheric market in a historic neighbourhood

A short stroll from historic Nollendorfplatz, Winterfeldtplatz and its Wednesday and Saturday markets are a salve to East Berlin's grit and grime. Take a seat at Moccas Café, right in the middle of the market, and bask in the sunshine surrounded by well-to-do middle-aged Germans (easily identifiable by their quirky spectacles) getting *angetüdelt* (lightly sozzled) on Aperol and Grauburgunder (Pinot Gris). Wander around the stalls and graze through gözleme and *Krabbenbrötchen* (bread rolls packed with delicious tiny shrimp). Once you've had your fill, head south to Goltzstrasse, where you'll find stunning tiled buildings, irresistible Scandi design pieces at Nordliebe and another contender for Berlin's best pizza at Sironi.

Schöneberg, 10781
Nearest station: Nollendorfplatz
winterfeldtplatz.winterfeldt-markt.de

67

VIKTORIAPARK

Sunsets and sledding on a historic site

Built on low-lying marshland, Berlin is remarkably flat. The highest hill is Kreuzberg, which gives the famous neighbourhood its name, and you'll find its peak, Viktoriapark, draped in a verdant green blanket. Known for its slopes (the site of fierce toboggan races in winter), Golgotha beer garden and a deceptively real-looking artificial mountain waterfall, Viktoriapark is also steeped in history. Previously known as Weinberg, when it was covered in wine-producing vines, the views from its 'summit' (it's only 66 metres high) inspired King Friedrich Wilhelm III to build a neo-Gothic war memorial here in 1818. Today, it's a perfect spot for sunset beers.

Katzbachstrasse, 10965
Nearest station: Platz der Luftbrücke

68

BOXHAGENER PLATZ

Always-buzzing square with Sunday flea market

All shops close on Sundays in Germany, which is why flea markets become the activity du jour. Box-enhagener Platz Markt is one of the classics, with stalls selling uncomfortable-looking black leather outfits and trestle tables that groan under the weight of italo disco vinyls, jars of organic honey and antique ceramics. Venture out into Brandenburg if you're on a serious mission, but for the casual Sunday thrifter, Boxi (as it's locally known) is slap-bang in the middle of a great area for restaurants, making a session of browsing, eating and drinking an easy win – head to Primitiv (no.85) for a gin basil smash so fresh it'll burn through the most sluggish hangover.

Boxhagener Platz, 10245
Nearest station: Samariterstrasse

69

TEUFELSBERG

Dilapidated spy station

Of all the things you'd expect to find sitting in a quiet forest in west Berlin, a phallic-shaped spy headquarters isn't one of them. This bizarre structure is an abandoned listening station previously run by the US National Security Agency to monitor East Germany during the Cold War – though today its mainly known for graffiti and the wild boars that roam nearby rather than state secrets. The building's interiors are accessible by entry fee, but it's worth undertaking the 80-metre ascent up Berlin's highest hill where Teufelsberg sits for unbeatable views over the city. In summer, cool off after the climb with a swim in nearby lake Teufelssee and an ice cream in Ökowerk, the former power plant-ecological centre and cafe – or visit in autumn to see the city bedecked in golden foliage.

Teufelsseechaussee 10, 14193
Nearest station: Messe Süd
teufelsberg-berlin.de

70

RÜDESHEIMER PLATZ

Leafy square with an annual wine festival

Lurking in deepest Wilmersdorf is sleepy Rüdesheimer Platz, which seems like a non-event for most of the year – until summer, when the Weinfest gets underway. From May to September, a wooden hut sets up shop on the square to sell wine from the Rhine region, with notably excellent Reisling. Pack up a picnic basket and use it to fend off competitors for the green plastic tables underneath the plane trees; the fight is worth it for the very affordable glasses of wine. Things tend to wind down early, but stalwart 1970s *Kneipe* Spinnrad is on-hand nearby to keep the good times (and the jugs of frothy pils) rolling.

Rüdesheimer Platz 6, 14197
Nearest station: Rüdesheimer Platz

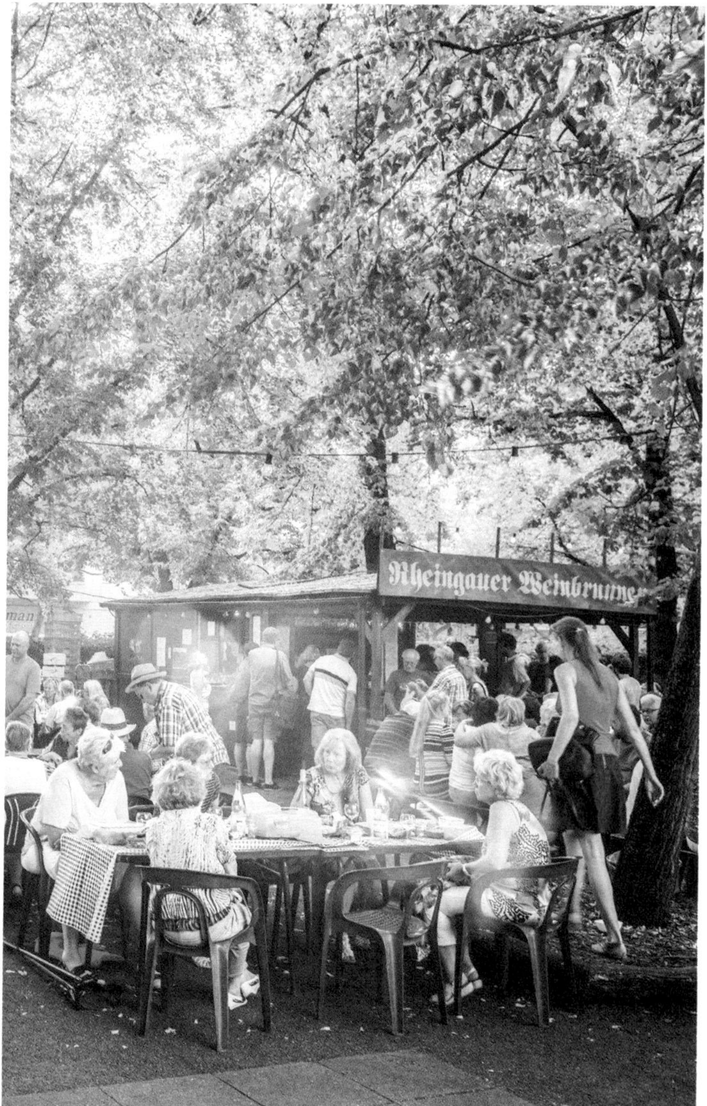
Rheingauer

71

VOLKSPARK REHBERGE

Sprawling wilderness and lively lido

More meadow than park, Rehberge's main appeal lies in its historic *Strandbad* (lido). With its 1920s edifice, sandy beaches, shady awnings and gently swaying hammocks, you could almost be on the Italian riviera, but the bass-heavy high BPMs from the DJ booth bring you back to Berlin with a bang. If you don't want to pay the entry fee, plenty of people sunbathe in the park itself for free. Elsewhere, there's an open-air theatre and cinema for balmy evenings, and the park's grassy expanse is laced by walking and cycling paths – just watch out for the wild boars.

Transvaalstrasse 160, 13351
Nearest station: Rehberge

72

VOLKSPARK HUMBOLDTHAIN

Rose garden beside a wartime bunker

You're never too far from the past in Berlin, but history sits in remarkably plain sight in this green space on the edge of Mitte. Stroll through the manicured rose garden and you'll soon notice two hulking grey structures jutting above the tree-tops ahead of you: a pair of World War II flak (anti-aircraft) towers that also served as bunkers. Today, you can scramble up serpentine pathways to ascend the 100 metres and reach the top of the hill, where you'll be rewarded with views over the city. The area even has a tiny vineyard that produces around 200 bottles of Humboldthainer Hauptstadtsekt sparkling wine a year, though you'll need to befriend a local councillor for a sip.

Brunnenstrasse, 13357
Nearest station: Gesundbrunnen

73

CAFÉ AM NEUEN SEE

Beautiful lakeside beer garden with boats

If you go down to the woods of Tiergarten today, you're sure of a big surprise: Berlin's not-so-secret hideaway, Café am Neuen See. Instead of a teddy bears' picnic, though, you'll find a beer garden by a lake, with inviting wooden decking and long tables perfect for grazing through an easy menu of wood-fired pizzas and seasonal German classics. On hot, humid summer days, one of the best ways to cool down is by renting a rowing boat and drifting out onto the glittering lake, which is an especially magical spot in the hazy *blaue Stunde* (twilight).

Lichtensteinallee 2, 10787
Nearest station: Wittenbergplatz
cafeamneuensee.de

74
HOTEL ODERBERGER

Neo-Renaissance grandeur

You wouldn't be alone in mistaking the grand Hotel Oderberger for a palace, but this imposing structure is a former *Stadtbad* (public swimming pool). These days, it also houses 70 bedrooms designed to preserve the building's unique character, with five small studios in the old water tower, where soaring ceilings amplify showstopping views over Berlin. The hotel lands you right in the middle of pretty Prenzlauer Berg, with its wide, boulevard-like cobbled streets providing the backdrop for a slew of tasting menu-style restaurants. The real draw at Oderberger is the pool, with its hanging lamps, cavernous, vaulted ceiling, arched columns and small but beautiful sauna – be warned: this is Germany, so nudity is actively encouraged.

Oderberger Strasse 57, 10435
Nearest station: Eberswalder Strasse
hotel-oderberger.berlin

75

LOCKE LIVING

Industrial-chic studios in a prime location

Sitting cheek by jowl with the East Side Gallery
(a surviving section of the Berlin Wall decorated
by artists), this aparthotel in Friedrichshain com-
bines the convenience of a hotel with the privacy
of a studio apartment, offering concrete-walled,
neutrally furnished studios by the River Spree.
There's a comfortable co-working space and a gym
overlooking the river, but Anima – the cafe and
restaurant – is more likely to catch your eye. A nod
to Japanese listening bars, it hosts regular music
nights, enhanced by a pale-wood sound system
repurposed from a 1970s Japanese cinema. In the
evening, a dressy, cosmopolitan crowd come to
graze on doorstop-sized wedges of springy bread
with burnt butter, steak tartare and an inventive,
umami-packed mushroom ravioli made with delicate slices of celeriac in place of pasta.

Mühlenstrasse 61–63, 10243
Nearest station: Warschauer Strasse
lockeliving.com

76

THE HOXTON, CHARLOTTENBURG

Elegant expression of West Berlin style

In a city known for its love of grey, black and endless cement, The Hoxton celebrates Berlin's 1920s heyday with Art Nouveau accents in the form of scalloped headboards, and a muted colour palette of pink and forest green. While the design feels distinctively 'Hoxton', there are lovely nods to the location in additions like the *Kamine* (chimney) in the Winter Garden – a conservatory-like space commonly found in Berlin flats. House of Tandoor is the on-site restaurant and boasts not one, but *three* copper tandoor ovens churning out puffy naan and whole, burnished cauliflowers, with a bar serving Indian-spiced, tea-infused takes on classic cocktails: here, the spritz is a reviving mix of iced tea, elderflower and champagne.

Meinekestrasse 18–19, 10719
Nearest station: Augsburger Strasse
thehoxton.com

77

THE MICHELBERGER

Fiercely independent hotel with farm-to-table food

The Michelberger is Berlin's original boutique hotel. Ten years after opening, it's still the leader of the pack, with dreamily squashy bedding, high-ceilinged rooms cleverly partitioned by pale-wood walls and large baths made all the better by the hotel's bespoke sweet orange bath products. Don't miss the restaurant downstairs (almost always booked out) or the breakfast buffet, both of which make use of a full rainbow of produce from the hotel's farm in Spreewald (where you can also stay the night, should that tickle your fancy). Beyond the hotel, you're in a great position from which to explore east Berlin – whether whiling away your Sunday at Boxhagener Platz's flea market (no.68) or late-night drinking in Club der Visionäre (no.81).

Warschauer Strasse 39–40, 10243
Nearest station: Warschauer Strasse
michelbergerhotel.com

78

WILMINA

Criminally stylish hotel

Wilmina has had quite the journey: where its towering walls once held a women's prison, they now house a luxurious hotel. There's more to the building's story than first meets the eye, and the rooms' original doors and bars over the windows offer a taster of its past. The labyrinthine white spaces may give a sanatorium-made-chic vibe, but they're filled with lovely touches, like an atrium adorned with Bocci lights and an infinite supply of fresh poppyseed cake in the communal kitchen. On the roof, you'll find a pocket-sized swimming pool (unheated, FYI) and a bookable private sauna. Don't miss Lovis, the discreet restaurant and bar serving unique drinks in long-stemmed glasses – No. 66, with sour cherry, almond and lemon, is crisp and addictive.

Kantstrasse 79, 10627
Nearest station: Charlottenburg
wilmina.com

79

BAR SWAY

Natural wines in living room-style surrounds

Founded by a group of friends who wanted to turn
their cosy evenings swilling natural wines at home
into a business, Bar Sway benefits from a team
with serious creative pedigree. Though meant to
evoke the feeling of visiting a friend's stylish flat,
the highly designed space is a few cuts above your
average living room, with nary a wonky clothes
drying rack in sight. You'll find graphic design by
Munich record label Public Possession, hand-built
speakers from H.A.N.D. HiFi and a sleek marble
counter with dark stools. There are eight rotating wines to try daily and a small menu of snacks,
featuring the king of all grilled cheese sandwiches
and one heck of pickle.

Pannierstrasse 29, 12047
Nearest station: Schönleinstrasse
bar-sway.com

80

HACKBARTH'S

Time-resistant Kneipe

For better or for worse, the unstoppable force of gentrification has taken hold of Berlin, and nowhere more so than in Mitte, where streets have been transformed by boutiques and chic restaurants. But you'll still find the city's free-wheeling spirit if you know where to look. Hackbarth's, in particular, is one such beacon of old-Berlin glamour. Part-*Kneipe*, part-coffee shop and housed in a former bakery in a Mitte backstreet, you can pitch up at the brass bar almost any time (it's open until the early hours) and find yourself surrounded by beret-wearing bohos drinking Riesling and freshly poured pils.

Auguststrasse 49A, 10119
Nearest station: Rosenthaler Platz

81

CLUB DER VISIONÄRE

Waterside bar/club known for house music

Waterside seating in the dappled light beneath a weeping willow makes for a pretty picturesque party location, but this is only one of Club der Visionäere's many USPs. On hot summer days you can dangle your feet in the water while you chat with friends to a soundtrack of the very best minimal house music. The chilled vibe makes this a popular spot for drinks and a few hours of dancing (rather than a weekend-long party). The location is also an ideal starting point for visitors: it forms part of the Arena Berlin complex, with other clubs Badeschiff, Hoppetosse and Glasshaus in easy reach. The result is an international crowd, but it's no less loved by Berliners.

Am Flutgraben 1, 12435
Nearest station: Schlesisches Tor
clubdervisionaere.com

82

YAAM

Celebrating Berlin's African community

In a city renowned for its techno scene, YAAM (Young African Arts Market) is a historic music venue and events space that's never been afraid to stand out. Originally founded as a cultural space for youth in 1994, it's since undergone several location changes and has grown into an institution representing diversity and African culture within the city. Hosting everything from basketball tournaments and gigs from the likes of Dele Sosimi to street art markets, everything takes place under the watchful eye of an iconic mural from Portuguese artist Vhils. The space recently secured its location for another 30 years; news that was hugely celebrated in Berlin's music and arts community.

Schillingbrücke 3, 10243
Nearest station: Ostbahnhof
yaam.de

83

MACKE PRINZ

Casual Berlin bar for late-night drinking

Perched on the edge of Zionskirchplatz, Macke Prinz is a lively take on the *Kneipe* (a no-frills dive bar often presented as Germany's answer to the British pub). They're a vital part of Berlin's drinking culture and often frequented by extremely grouchy Berliners. This one is filled with slightly more amiable 20- to 30-somethings drinking and snacking on dangerously moreish *Salzstäbchen* (pretzel sticks) until the bleary hours of the morning. Macke Prinz is one of Berlin's smoker-friendly bars, so beware of sporting your slickest outfit as there's a slight possibility you'll feel like you've woken up in an ashtray the next morning – but what would Berlin be without its gritty allure?

Zionskirchstrasse 39, 10119
Nearest station: Rosenthaler Platz

84

MÖBEL OLFE

Boisterous Kreuzberg gay bar

Kottbusser Tor, more affectionately known as Koti, is one of Berlin's most richly diverse neighbourhoods, ringed by satellite dish-adorned high-rises, bars and plenty of kebab shops (word on the street is that Doyum's döner is the best). On the ground floor of the Brutalist 1960s housing estate that dominates the central roundabout, you'll recognise popular gay spot Möbel Olfe by the bodies pressed right up against the floor-to-ceiling windows. The energy is always high – which could have something to do with the astonishingly cheap drinks – and you'll spy old sofas fixed to the walls that are a nod to its former life as a furniture store. The bar itself is the real focal point, honouring its Koti location with an army of satellite dishes turned into a trippy space mosaic of light fixtures.

Reichenberger Strasse 177, 10999
Nearest station: Kottbuser Tor
moebel-olfe.de

85

PRIMITIV BAR

Superb cocktails in a simple setting

The classic Berlin bar is characterised by litre jugs of pils, low lighting, rickety flea market-sourced furniture and those red glass candle holders found in dive bars worldwide. This isn't a bad thing; it's just Berlin's particular brand of cool, and with any luck it'll never change. Primitiv fits this bill down to a T but stands out from the crowd with an extensive list of classic and inventive cocktails, an impressive collection of rare spirits and extremely reasonable prices. The bar, a few streets behind buzzing Boxhagener Platz (no.68), is always full-to-bursting. You'll have to be quick to get a seat, particularly on the regular burlesque nights that turn the tiny stage, into a glittery, streamer-bedecked wonderland.

Simon-Dach-Strasse 28, 10245
Nearest station: Warschauer Strasse

86

WAX ON

World-class drinks with experimental mixology

In a city dominated by *Kneipe* (affordable late-night drinking dens), cocktail enthusiasts have been thirsty for something different. Enter Wax On, elevating the game with rotary evaporators, centrifuges and a commitment to cocktail perfection so intense, if you pop to the toilet they'll whisk your drink away and put it in the fridge to stay cool. The man behind it is bartender Sam Orrock (who cut his teeth at London favourite Scout), and it's been such a success that it recently smashed into the World's 50 Best Bars at number 29. Perch at an industrial-chic plastic table and order the house sour, made with almond, chai, black walnut and lemon, or Go Apes, with clarified banana and soda.

Weserstrasse 208, 12047
Nearest station: Hermannplatz
instagram.com/waxonberlin

87

://ABOUT BLANK

Stalwart club with outdoor dancefloor

Berlin's clubbing scene makes up a large part of the city's cultural map and is a fiercely protected space for freedom and self-expression. Berghain is usually the name on visitors' lips, but you can avoid the notorious queue by looking to the city's other clubs – and in the process develop a fuller picture of Berlin's nightlife. ://about blank, a hop and a skip from Ostkreuz station, has several rooms playing a variety of techno, house and other electronic music, and a much-loved outdoor dancefloor. The monthly Staub parties have a devoted following, and if you find yourself especially enamoured, you can buy everything from T-shirts to babygrows emblazoned with the club's infamous broken-down campervan.

Markgrafendamm 24c, 10245
Nearest station: Ostkreuz
aboutblank.li

88

OHM

Intimate club with pioneering curation

OHM is little sister and neighbour to techno giant Tresor, the legendary club first founded in the vaults of a Berlin department store in 1991. Today, both OHM and Tresor occupy the ground-floor of Kraftwerk, a concrete-walled former power plant on Köpenicker Strasse with yawning spaces ideal for accommodating hundreds of bodies. Where Tresor is sprawling, OHM is intimate; nights revolve around one DJ stage and the neon-lit, white-tiled bar, creating a more open, friendly feel than a super-club. The programming also caters for eclectic tastes and is keenly tracked by audiophiles; go on Thursday for a more experimental vibe, or the self-explanatory Techno Tuesdays.

Köpenicker Strasse 70, 10179
Nearest station: Heinrich-Heine-Strasse
ohmberlin.com

IMAGE CREDITS

An Opinionated Guide to Berlin
First edition

Published in 2024
by Hoxton Mini Press, London
Copyright © Hoxton Mini Press 2024.
All rights reserved.

Text by Lydia Winter
Editing by Zoë Jellicoe
Design and production
by Richard Mason
Proofreading by Florence Ward
Editorial support by Leona Crawford

With thanks to Matthew Young for
initial series design.

Please note: we recommend checking
the websites listed for each entry
before you visit for the latest
information on price, opening times
and pre-booking requirements.

Thank you to all of the individuals
and institutions who have provided
images and arranged permissions.
While every effort has been made to
trace the present copyright holders
we apologise in advance for any
unintentional omission or error,
and would be pleased to insert the
appropriate acknowledgement in any
subsequent edition.

A CIP catalogue record for this book
is available from the British Library.

ISBN: 978-1-914314-73-5

Printed and bound by OZGraf, Poland

Hoxton Mini Press is an environmen-
tally conscious publisher, committed
to offsetting our carbon footprint.
This book is 100 per cent carbon
compensated, with offset purchased
from Stand For Trees.

Every time you order from our
website, we plant a tree:
www.hoxtonminipress.com

MIX
Paper | Supporting
responsible forestry
FSC® C163799

INDEX